Rookie reader®

Circle City

Written by
Dana Meachen Rau

Illustrated by
Susan Miller

CHILDREN'S PRESS®
A Division of Grolier Publishing
New York London Hong Kong Sydney
Danbury, Connecticut

For Charlie
—D.M.R.

For Lili
—S.M.

READING CONSULTANTS
Linda Cornwell
Coordinator of School Quality and Professional Improvement
(Indiana State Teachers Association)

Katharine A. Kane
Education Consultant
(Retired, San Diego County Office of Education and San Diego State University)

Visit Children's Press® on the Internet at:
http://publishing.grolier.com

Library of Congress Cataloging-in-Publication Data
Rau, Dana Meachen.
  Circle city / written by Dana Meachen Rau ; illustrated by Susan Miller.
    p. cm.—(Rookie reader)
  Summary: A child points out all the circles she sees while out walking, from car
and bus tires to coins and pizza.
  ISBN 0-516-21632-5 [lib. bdg.]   0-516-26543-1 [pbk.]
  1. Circle—Juvenile literature. [1. Circle.] I. Miller, Susan, ill. II. Title. III. Series.
QA484.R38 1999
516'.15—dc21   98-53055
                                                         CIP
                                                         AC

GROLIER
PUBLISHING

I live in circle city!
I see circles everywhere!

Circles on cars.
Circles on buses.

Circles in my pocket.

Circles
in stores.

Circles in the park.

Circles to buy.

Circles in the sky.

Circles on the ground.

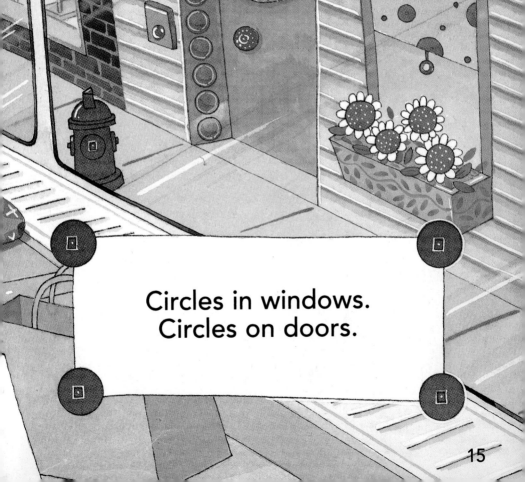

Circles in windows.
Circles on doors.

Circles
to eat.

19

Circles to play.

21

I live in circle city.

Word List (25 words)

buses
buy
cars
circle
circles
city
doors
eat
everywhere
ground
I
in
live

my
on
park
play
pocket
push
see
sky
stores
the
to
windows

About the Author

Dana Meachen Rau is the author of many books for children, including *A Box Can Be Many Things*, *The Secret Code*, *Purple Is Best*, and *Bob's Vacation* (which she also illustrated) in the Rookie Reader series. She has always studied both writing and art, and loves crafting words and pictures into the perfect story. She also works as a children's book editor and looks for circles with her husband, Chris, and son, Charlie, in Farmington, Connecticut.

About the Illustrator

Susan Miller has been a freelance children's illustrator for more than ten years and has illustrated numerous books and materials for children. She works in her home studio in the rural Litchfield Hills of Connecticut, where she lives with her husband and two school-age children. They provide her endless opportunities for inspiration. She has also illustrated *Nana's Hog* and *Cowboy Up!* in the Rookie Reader series.